$10

EX-LIB

- 1968 -

OUT OF PRINT

HOKUSAI

Biographies by Elizabeth Ripley

HOKUSAI
COPLEY
RODIN
BOTTICELLI
DURER
GAINSBOROUGH
PICASSO
RAPHAEL
TITIAN
WINSLOW HOMER
LEONARDO DA VINCI
MICHELANGELO
REMBRANDT
RUBENS
GOYA
VAN GOGH
VELAZQUEZ

HOKUSAI

A Biography

by Elizabeth Ripley

J. B. LIPPINCOTT COMPANY

Philadelphia   New York

ACKNOWLEDGMENTS

I wish to thank Miss Emily Biederman of the Boston Museum of Fine Arts, who spent many hours helping me to choose illustrations for this book. I acknowledge thanks to the Charles E. Tuttle Company for permitting me to use quotations from *The Hokusai Sketchbooks* edited by James A. Michener. I am indebted to the staff of the Fernald Library of Colby Junior College for allowing me to write in their quiet Reading Room.

My thanks to Chitose Tanaka and the six members of the Tokyo Police Force who devoted one morning helping me to locate Hokusai's grave in Tokyo; and to my sister, Eunice Bohanon, for her assistance in procuring photographs, her helpful advice, and for her services as guide and companion in Japan.

ILLUSTRATIONS

Facing Page

ASAKUSA SHRINE, EDO   6

FOUR COURTESANS OF THE HOUSE OF CHOJIYA   8

SEYAWA KIKUJURO ACTING WOMAN'S PART   10

ACTOR DANJURŌ   10

CHINESE BOYS AT PLAY   12

A FERRYBOAT WITH PASSENGERS
   BEARING NEW YEAR'S GIFTS   14

LADY AND ATTENDANTS   16

ATTACK ON MORANOA'S CASTLE   18

ARMORER'S SHOP   20

A SPRING SCENE AT SHINMEI SHRINE OF SHIBA   20

PORTRAIT OF THE ARTIST   22

SHOWER AT SHIN-YANGI BRIDGE   24

RIDER AND ESCORTS IN RAIN   24

CHINESE TORTURES   26

Drawings from *Quick Lessons in Simplified Drawing*   28

ANIMALS   30

WORKMEN MAKING ROPE, NOODLES, LENSES
   AND UMBRELLAS   32

LANDSCAPE WITH PAGODAS   34

THIN PEOPLE   36

ACROBATS   38

LANDSCAPE OF ARMY IN SNOW   40

FAT MEN   42

MICE   44

FAMOUS CALLIGRAPHERS   46

MOUNT FUJI SEEN FROM EJIRI   48

THE GREAT WAVE   50

AMIDA WATERFALL   52

HANGING BRIDGE   54

WISTERIA AND WAGTAIL   56

CHRYSANTHEMUMS   58

WARRIOR COMBATTING PHANTOM   60

WORSHIPPERS AT THE FOOT OF FUJI   62

SELF-PORTRAIT   64

WILLOW AND YOUNG CROWS   66

A FAGGOT GATHERER   68

One spring day a little boy trotted on short plump legs along the streets of Edo. He dodged salesmen with baskets which were suspended from bamboo poles across their shoulders, paused for a moment as three priests carrying a temple bell passed by, then suddenly dove across the street between the hooves of a galloping horse into the open doorway of a bookshop. The owner smiled as the boy, standing on tiptoes, examined a pile of brightly colored picture prints, for he knew that Tokitara always treated books and pictures with the greatest care.

That evening Tokitara jogged along the river bank lined with cherry trees to his home. He gulped down the bowlful of rice his mother gave him, then squatted on his heels in front of a blank piece of paper. Holding an ink-filled brush so that the fine point barely touched the paper he drew the outline of a bird in flight. Hour after hour the six-year-old boy sat bent over his paper, his thatch of straight black hair falling over his dark shiny eyes. Slowly and steadily he guided his brush, bringing to life flowers, animals, and people he had seen in Edo.

Sometimes he watched his father engraving designs on the backs of mirrors, which he sold to the Shogun, or military ruler of Japan. One day he picked up an engraver's tool and found that he was able to cut clean lines in metal.

When Tokitara was fourteen his father sent him to an engraver's workshop. For four years the boy cut woodblocks from other artists' drawings so that they could be printed many times.

Then, in 1778, he joined the studio of the popular print designer, Shunshō. So quickly did he learn to imitate his master's style, that, according to Japanese custom, he was allowed to adopt part of the older artist's name. But Tokitara, now called Shunrō, did not always copy Shunsho's formal style. One of his prints showed a busy scene in front of an Edo temple, where ladies and gentlemen and their servants strolled about the courtyard or bargained with salesmen in their booths. This informal picture was quite unlike the master's stylized compositions, but Tokitara proudly signed it with his new name *Shunrō*.

ASAKUSA SHRINE, EDO

About 1780. Wood-block Print. (10⅜″ × 15⅛″)

Collection S. Watanabe, Tokyo

Shunrō's master soon regretted that he had allowed his eccentric pupil to adopt his name. He had to admit that the genial boy was clever. After years of studying prints in bookshops, Shunrō was able to imitate the styles of many artists. Some of his vigorous black and white prints were so different from his teacher's delicately colored pictures that the master, Shunshō, became enraged. If Shunrō continued to imitate the vulgar artists he would be dismissed. Shunrō smiled and continued to experiment with different styles.

He never complained about being poor. All he needed was a bowl of rice, a straw mat to sleep on, and time to draw. He hoped he would live to be a hundred so that he could perfect his skill. He knew that many of his prints were poor, for he was made to work so quickly. Every year the Shunshō workshop turned out hundreds of wood-block prints which the people of Edo could buy for just one penny. There were portraits of popular actors, illustrations of the most recent plays and fashion plates of the latest styles. These prints were designed in the formal manner of the master. One of Shunrō's fashion plates showed four willowy ladies in kimonos. Their elaborately dressed hair, heavily lacquered, was stuck full of combs and fancy hairpins. One of the ladies, holding a brush, wrote a letter, while the other three looked on.

FOUR COURTESANS OF THE HOUSE OF CHOJIYA

1782. Wood-block Print. (14″ × 9⅛″)

British Museum, London

There was always great excitement when a traveling theater visited Edo, and Shunrō usually managed to scrape together enough money to buy a ticket. The play began at sunrise and lasted until it grew too dark to see the stage. The plots, taken from Japanese history or mythology, were familiar, and the audience applauded wildly when their favorite actors stamped about the stage, managing their long robes so skillfully that the trains fell in strikingly angular folds about their feet. Some actors played fierce warriors wielding swords, some terrifying ghosts, and others stately women, for Japanese women were not allowed to act.

One popular actor of women's parts was Kikujuro. Prints of his portrait by Shunrō appeared soon after he performed in Edo. Following the rigid formula of his master, Shunrō fitted the actor's figure into a tall narrow panel, for portrait prints of actors must, like playing cards, be of equal size. But Shunrō seldom observed the other monotonous rules laid down by his master. In vain Shunshō lashed out at his assistant for imitating the vulgar school called Kano, or for drawing tall willowy ladies like those of his rival Utamaro. If his pupil insisted on signing his prints "Shunrō," he must follow Shunshō's rules.

The partnership lasted for eight stormy years, until one of Shunshō's pupils told his master that he had seen a Shunrō poster in the Kano style hanging over a picture dealer's door. In a rage the pupil had torn the picture to pieces while Shunrō looked on calmly.

Shunshō's face grew crimson. This was the final insult to the workshop. Shunrō was told to pack up his brushes and leave the school forever.

Shunrō tucked his bundle of brushes under his arm and strolled contentedly along the street. He was glad that his master had expelled him, for he had learned all that he needed to know about wood-block printing. Now, at twenty-six, he would begin to perfect his drawing.

He found a job illustrating comic books, which paid him so little that he could not always buy his daily rice. Finally he became so hungry that he decided to earn his rice by peddling red peppers on the street. Many people stopped the genial salesman to examine his baskets filled with peppers and the gaily colored almanacs which dangled from a bamboo pole across his shoulder. Few suspected that this smiling peddler longed to be an artist. Once when Shunrō spotted his old teacher in the crowd he ducked across the street, not wishing Shunshō to know that he could not make a living from his art.

A) SEYAWA KIKUJURO ACTING WOMAN'S PART

1783. Wood-block Print. (11⅜″ × 5⅜″)

Courtesy, Museum of Fine Arts, Boston

Gift of William Sturgis Bigelow

B) ACTOR DANJURŌ

1784. Wood-block Print. (12⅛″ × 5¼″)

British Museum, London

But Shunrō's talent was not forgotten. Three years after he had been expelled, a friend commissioned him to design a banner for the Festival of Boys. He was paid so well that suddenly he felt rich. That day he vowed that he would devote his life to art.

He soon found a publisher for his prints which showed Chinese boys at play. In one, a boy rode a hobbyhorse, another held an umbrella, a third a banner, and three more were playing tug-of-war.

Shunrō's reputation grew. He was asked to assist another artist who was restoring a temple in the town of Nikko. The artists set off together, stopping at inns along the way. One innkeeper commissioned Shunrō's employer to paint a picture for his room and board. When Shunrō saw the painting he smiled and shook his head. The picture showed a boy knocking down fruit from a tree with a bamboo pole. Why, asked Shunrō, had the artist shown the boy on tiptoes when the pole reached far above the fruit? The employer glared at his assistant. If Shunrō couldn't understand that the boy was placed on tiptoes purposely, to show that he was clumsy, his helper need not continue on to Nikko.

Shunrō tossed his bundle across his shoulder and returned to Edo.

CHINESE BOYS AT PLAY

1789. Wood-block Print. (14¼″ × 9½″)

Courtesy, Museum of Fine Arts, Boston

William S. and John T. Spaulding Collection

Only rich people could afford greeting cards in Japan, for each was designed according to the instructions of the sender. These made-to-order cards, or *surinomos*, announced marriages, births, or changes of name which occurred frequently in Japan. The customer specified how the artist should illustrate an invitation to a concert or a poetry reading. Some of the long tall surinomos announced retirements or changes of address, and many were designed as New Year's greetings.

Shunrō's surinomos, unlike his strongly colored prints, were delicately tinted cards in the style of the artist Sōri, so once more Shunrō decided to take another artist's name. One of his New Year's cards, signed "Sōri," showed a boatload of passengers sailing into port, bearing gifts.

The surinomos brought in little money, but Sōri decided he could afford to marry. His wife tried not to worry about being poor. She marketed, cooked, and scrubbed, while Sōri sat on his heels, hour after hour, turning out drawings which he threw on the floor around him. When his wife complained because she was not allowed to clean the cluttered room, Sōri solved the problem by moving to another house.

One day Sōri returned to his house with a roll of drawings which, he explained, had been ordered by a Dutch sea captain who had refused to pay the price agreed on. Sōri's wife, tired and hungry, could not hide her rage. Didn't her husband realize that they were poor? He should have sold the pictures at any price, for no one would buy these drawings in Japan. But the more she scolded the more Sōri insisted that he would make the foreigner keep his bargain. Some weeks later the captain agreed to pay Sōri's price and, before he left Japan, he ordered more drawings to take back to Holland. Soon Sōri's pictures of Japanese life were selling by the hundreds. Then suddenly the sale was stopped. The Shogun, suspicious that the foreign merchants would learn defense secrets from the pictures, forbade them to export Sōri's drawings.

A FERRYBOAT WITH PASSENGERS BEARING NEW YEAR'S GIFTS

About 1800. Surinomo. (8″ × 21⅛″)
Courtesy, Museum of Fine Arts, Boston

Once in a while some richly dressed gentleman called at Sōri's studio to order a painting for his house. Sōri would bow and scrape as the wealthy client described in detail what he wanted. The gentleman had given time and thought to this picture which would be the only decoration on the walls of his sparsely furnished house and, because it would not be reproduced by wood block, the artist was free to use as many delicate shades of color as he wished.

Sōri worked on these paintings, called *kakemonos*, with the greatest care. First he made quick brush sketches. Then, for hours he contemplted a blank piece of silk on which the painting would be made. When he knew exactly where he would place each line, he picked up his brush and began to paint. As the silk absorbed the exquisite shades of color which ran from the tip of his pointed brush, a picture of a tall, willowy lady and her attendants came to life. Above the figures he wrote a description of the picture, then signed his name, "Sōri," in the lower right-hand corner.

In 1779, Sōri moved with his wife and children to another part of Edo. Because his new studio was now in the northern section of the city, Sōri decided to change his name to "Hokusai," which meant "Star of the Northern Constellation."

LADY AND ATTENDANTS

About 1779. Painting on silk. (33¾″ × 13″)

Courtesy, Museum of Fine Arts, Boston

Ever since he was a boy Hokusai had heard tales about the forty-seven wandering knights called *Ronin*. Some of these tales were true, and others only legends, but everyone in Japan had heard the thrilling story of these heroes who had lived one hundred years before.

The story began at the Shogun's court which was preparing for the yearly visit of the Emperor's ambassador from Kyoto. According to court custom, two lords had been chosen to receive the imperial visitor, and a tutor appointed to teach the lords the proper etiquette. This year the tutor, who was cruel and overbearing, demanded that his pupils pay for their instruction with expensive presents. When one of the lords refused to offer bribes, he was punished unmercifully by his teacher. Unable to bear the insults any longer, the lord drew his sword and struck the tutor.

In Japan, the penalty for this crime was death. The lord, according to court rules, was ordered to kill himself with his sword. The lord's retainers, finding themselves without a master, vowed to avenge his death.

For years the forty-seven Ronin wandered about the country, hungry and penniless, while they plotted how they would kill the tutor. One winter night the knights secretly entered the tutor's castle and cut off the villain's head. The lord had been avenged; but the penalty for the knight's crime was, like their master's, death. The next day forty-seven Ronin plunged their swords into their sides and died.

Stories and poems were written about the Ronin until they became the most popular heroes in Japan. Hundreds of prints were designed which told different stories about these venerated knights. Whenever a new Ronin play was shown in Edo, Hokusai designed a set of prints which illustrated each scene.

The most exciting scene was the attack on the tutor's castle. The Ronin, having quietly entered the castle courtyard, attacked the guards with the weapons they had made in exile. One shot arrows from a roof, another wielded a sword, and another a long spear. One knight with a shield and sword broke into a room where the tutor, dressed in nightclothes, held up his arms in terror.

ATTACK ON MORANOA'S CASTLE

From Act XI of *Chusingura* (Forty-seven Ronin)

1789–1806. Wood-block Print. (9¼″ × 13¾″)

Courtesy, Museum of Fine Arts, Boston

Hokusai loved to explore Edo. Every day he found new, amusing subjects for his sketchbook. He sat on the docks watching men winding enormous strands of rope and was impressed by the strength and vitality of these workmen. He investigated all kinds of workshops, sketching what he saw. He drew women seated on the floor in front of an open drum in which they were grinding rice with tall bamboo poles. He watched men pounding rice cakes with heavy mallets, and carpenters sawing and planing wood. The quieter shops intrigued him, too. He sketched doll shops, food shops, and the print shops which he had always loved to visit.

In 1800, Hokusai's sketches were published in a book. *Amusements of the Eastern Capital* took the readers on a tour of Edo. They looked into the doorway of an armorer's shop where two little dogs were sitting. Inside a workman was busily hammering out a suit of armor which was hanging on a form. Displayed on a rack against the wall were ornately decorated saddles.

The reader was shown views of well-known shrines. One, set in a landscape of pine-covered hills, was popular with tourists. On spring days crowds strolled about the vast courtyard outside the temple, and many stopped to buy food and souvenirs at little stands shaded by umbrellas.

The people of Edo were delighted with Hokusai's guidebook. Workers and peasants, who could not read, pored over pictures of familiar scenes. The book was so successful that the publisher asked for more; but before a second guidebook was ready for the printer, Hokusai's first novel appeared in the Edo bookshops.

A) ARMORER'S SHOP
   From *Amusements of the Eastern Capital*
   1802
   Courtesy, Museum of Fine Arts, Boston
   Gift of Mrs. J. K. Morse

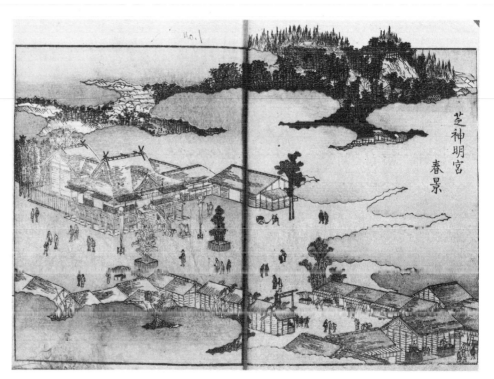

B) A SPRING SCENE AT SHINMEI SHRINE OF SHIBA
   From *Amusements of the Eastern Capital*
   1800
   Courtesy, Museum of Fine Arts, Boston

"I am sending to you my poor fiction," wrote Hokusai to a publisher.

"If this can be of any use to you, please publish it after your inspection." Below he drew a picture of himself kneeling before a table on which rolls of manuscripts were piled. His head was shaved according to the custom of artists and writers in Japan. With a few strokes of his brush he had captured an expression of false humility. His eyes were lowered and his mouth twisted in a wry smile.

"As this is my first attempt please ask the master . . . Bakin to correct my errors," he continued. Humbly he begged the best fiction writer in Japan to criticize his work.

But Hokusai did not feel as humble as he appeared.

"If this (book) has any success this year," he wrote, "I shall try again next spring and present the results to you."

The Tactics of General Oven told an amusing story about the financial troubles of a merchant. The plot was long and rambling, but the publisher knew that the author's illustrations would sell the book. When the novel was published the author's letter and portrait appeared on the last page.

Hokusai's novels did not bring him fame, but the author found other ways to attract the attention of the public. When he was chosen to paint a picture for a religious feast day, hundreds of people gathered outside the Buddhist temple to watch Hokusai perform. Many climbed to the temple roof in order to see the enormous sheet of paper spread on the ground before the artist. They watched silently as Hokusai dipped his brush, the size of a broom, into a bowlful of paint and swept it in wide strokes about the paper. Soon the head and shoulders of a Buddha filled the space. A horse could have passed through the god's mouth, and a man would have fitted into an eye.

When the picture was hoisted on a scaffolding for everyone to see, the audience went wild with joy.

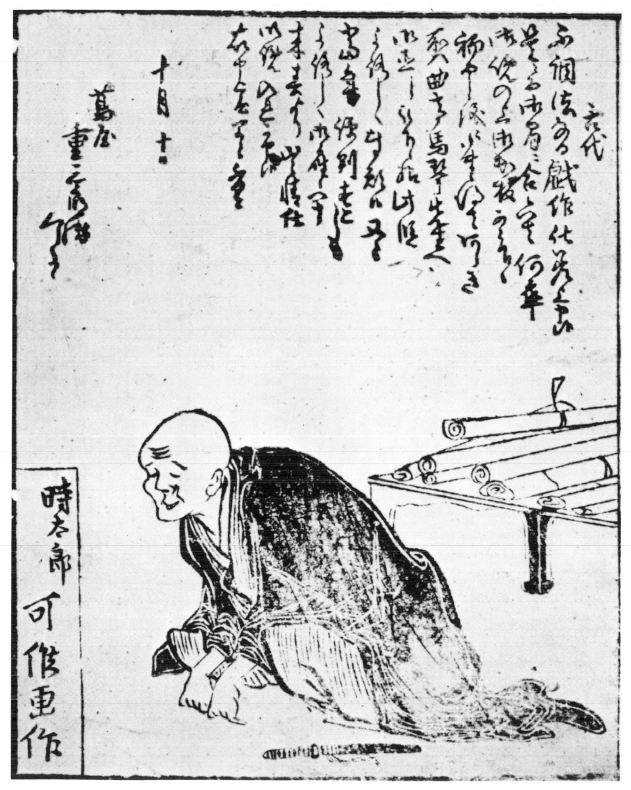

PORTRAIT OF THE ARTIST. From *The Tactics of General Oven*
1800

Photograph, Courtesy, New York Public Library

Each time Hokusai performed in Edo he showed his skill in some new way. Once he drew birds in flight on a grain of rice, and another time, instead of a brush he used an egg. More and more people talked about the amazing feats of the eccentric artist, and soon the Shogun invited him to give a performance at the palace.

The act did not last long. Hokusai spread his materials on the ground before the Shogun—an enormous sheet of paper, a broom-size brush, bowls of red and blue paint, and a rooster in a cage. In a few minutes he brushed light blue watercolor waves across the paper, then, before the color dried, he unlocked the cage, dipped the rooster's feet in bright red paint and let it run across the paper. This, he said, bowing low before the Shogun, was a picture of red maple leaves floating down the river.

Hokusai spent many hours walking along the banks of the Sumida River which ran through Edo. He sketched it at all times of year and from many places. In 1803 his pictures of this river were published in book form. This guidebook, called *Both Banks of the Sumida River at a Glance*, showed people strolling along banks lined with cherry trees, or picking their way in clogs along snow-covered paths. One page pictured people, surprised by a sudden shower, struggling across a bridge in pelting rain.

Hokusai also sketched the views outside the "Eastern Capital." His set of prints, called *Fifty-three Stations of the Tokaido Road*, pictured familiar landmarks on this important highway which connected the Shogun's capital, Edo, with the Emperor's capital, Kyoto. Every day gentlemen borne in litters, knights on horseback, and men on foot carrying heavy burdens passed along the Tokaido Road. Hokusai's prints showed this procession climbing steep winding paths, fording streams and riding through driving rain. Some pictured well-known stopping places along the way.

These prints, like the guidebooks, were popular with the working people, but because the price was low, Hokusai made little money on his work.

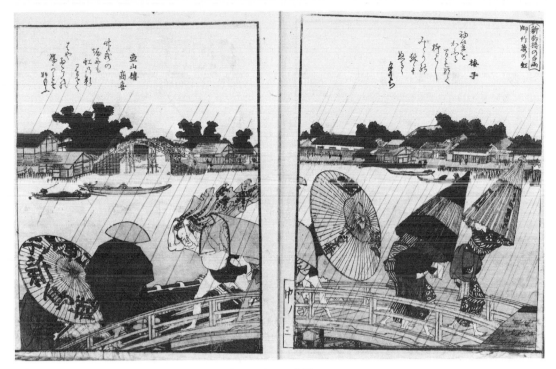

A) SHOWER AT SHIN-YANGI BRIDGE.
From *Both Banks of the Sumida River*
1803
Courtesy, Museum of Fine Arts, Boston
Gift of Edward S. Morse

B) RIDER AND ESCORTS IN RAIN. From *Tokaido Road* Series
1806. *Wood-block Print.* ($4\frac{5}{8}$" × $6\frac{7}{8}$")
Courtesy, Museum of Fine Arts, Boston
Gift of William Sturgis Bigelow

In 1807, the greatest novelist in Japan asked Hokusai to illustrate his books. Bakin's stories were filled with murders, tortures, and terrifying ghosts, which Hokusai interpreted as he wished. The artist who had once humbly begged Bakin to criticize his story, now did not hesitate to tell the author how to write; and Bakin stormed and fumed because the artist paid no attention to the text.

One day Bakin objected because Hokusai had not shown a character holding a shoe in his mouth.

"That is impossible," Hokusai replied, but Bakin insisted that it could be done.

"Try it then!" retorted Hokusai, and kept on drawing.

Author and artist fought and argued for four stormy years, while the publisher sold volume after volume of Bakin's novels illustrated by Hokusai. The artist claimed that the books were successful because of the illustrations, and Bakin answered angrily that without his text there would be no books.

Ten volumes of a Chinese story had just been completed when the great explosion came. Bakin refused to finish the work with Hokusai as illustrator, and Hokusai announced that he wouldn't continue with the illustrations unless the publisher found another author. The publisher debated and decided that the pictures were more important than the text. A less talented writer translated the remaining eighty volumes which Hokusai continued to illustrate as he wished.

A) and B) CHINESE TORTURES. From *Cruelties of Dobki*
About 1807
Courtesy, Museum of Fine Arts, Boston
Gift of Edward S. Morse

Hokusai's brush, sensitive to the slightest pressure moved slowly and steadily as it outlined geometric shapes. On one sheet he drew a circle, a few straight lines, several arcs of different sizes and a triangle. This combination of shapes was a simplified drawing of the goat which Hokusai had placed beside it. On the right he had outlined two overlapping circles, two parallel curves, two small arcs, and a few straight lines. This was a kind of diagram showing how to draw a horse. Hokusai, who drew these geometric shapes freehand, wanted to show how, with ruler and compass, anyone could teach himself to draw. He even dotted the spots where the point of the compass should be placed. On another page he illustrated how to load and hold a brush in order to make a fine dark line, and how to produce a graded tone, by spreading the bristles on the paper.

Hokusai's how-to book on drawing was a great success. Artists followed the simple rules, hoping to learn the secret of Hokusai's great skill. But Hokusai knew that he possessed a talent that no one else could copy. Everything he drew, he noted, seemed to be alive.

"I perceive that my people, animals, insects and fish appear to run away," he wrote in the preface to his book.

"Happily the engraver (of his drawings) took upon himself to cut with his well sharpened knife the veins and nerves of the beings I drew and deprived them of their ability to escape."

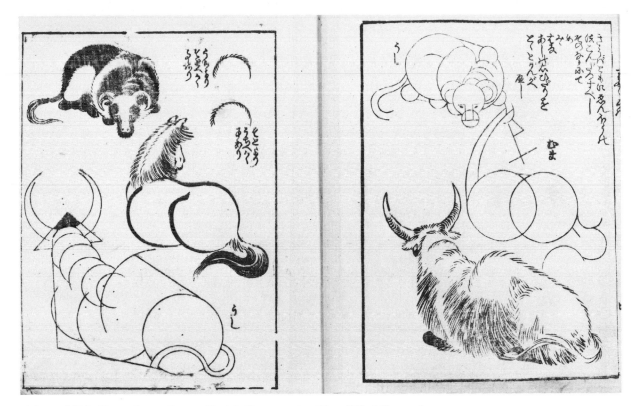

A) and B) Drawings from *Quick Lessons in Simplified Drawing*

1812

Courtesy, Museum of Fine Arts, Boston

Gift of William Sturgis Bigelow

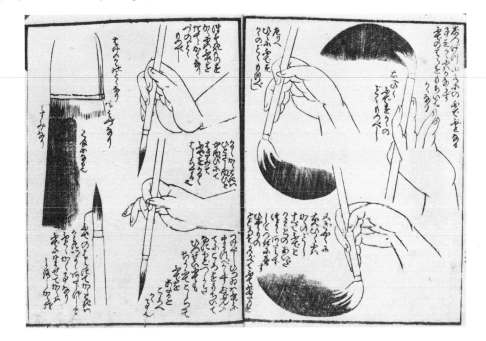

In the fall of 1812 Hokusai set off for the city of Nagoya. He was recognized by many as he traveled along the Tokaido Road, and was asked to perform stunts in drawing at some of the stopping places along the way. When he reached Nagoya he received a cordial welcome. He visited one fellow artist for six months.

His host entertained the master by giving sketching parties at his house. These were gay occasions. Sitting around a low table the artists sipped tea and made drawings of any subject which came to mind. Hokusai turned out hundreds of sketches, which he threw on the floor around him. There were drawings of children and birds, animals and trees, priests and workers, plants and buildings. His friends, marveling at his skill, urged him to publish his sketches in a book.

Soon engravers were hard at work cutting wood blocks from the master's drawings. When the publisher asked the artist to name a title for the book, Hokusai answered simply, "*Manga*," which, in Japanese, means "random sketches."

Three years later Hokusai's *Manga* appeared in many bookstalls in Japan. The working people flocked to buy the book which cost so little and was filled with lively sketches of every aspect of their life. The preface, written by an artist friend, described the contents of the book.

"The things of heaven and of Buddha, the life of men and women, even birds and beasts, plants and trees, and under his brush every phase and form of existence has arisen."

Readers nodded and giggled as they pored over pictures of familiar animals. On one page were three long-armed monkeys hanging from a limb. This arrangement, made in iron, was often used in Japan to hang lanterns from a ceiling. On the right, were tigers which Hokusai had seen in the Edo zoo. Below were squirrels, mice, and horses, and a strange mythological beast, part cow, part horse, with a turtle's shell on its back.

ANIMALS. From the *Manga*, Volume 1

1814

The Metropolitan Museum of Art, New York

Gift of Howard Mansfield, 1936

"How wonderful! How fascinating!" wrote a well-known poet in the preface to the second volume of the *Manga*. Here were drawings of dragons, birds and fish and, wrote the poet, "all kinds of people in all kinds of situations."

On one page two men stretched and twisted rope. Two more were making noodles; one trampled on dough sandwiched between straw mats, while the other rolled it on a board. A fortune-teller, squatting on the ground, examined a smug customer through a glass, and a lens maker ground lenses, while his customer held a telescope to his eye. At the bottom of the page three men made umbrellas. One decorated the covering, another split bamboo ribs, and a third mixed rice paste.

The day laborers of Edo were the models for these drawings. Hokusai, himself a craftsman, loved the working people who were his customers and friends. Although he moved from house to house, he always settled in a poor section of the city. A sign on his door read "peasant," to show that he came from the working class.

Hokusai, who was never impressed by riches, did not always take his important clients seriously.

"It is no use bowing and scraping or bringing me bribes," he wrote above his studio door.

One day Hokusai was picking fleas from his kimono, when a representative of the Shogun called and was told that the artist was far too busy to receive a visitor. The client waited patiently until he was finally admitted to the filthy studio. Horrified by the dirt and clutter, he completed his mission as quickly as he could. Hokusai grinned as he bowed his customer to the door, then pointing to the disordered room, begged the client to inform the Shogun that Hokusai's studio was the cleanest in the city.

WORKMEN MAKING ROPE, NOODLES, LENSES AND UMBRELLAS.
From the *Manga*, Volume 2.

1815

The Metropolitan Museum of Art, New York

Gift of Howard Mansfield, 1936

"The master . . . has made random sketches of everything," wrote the author in his preface to the fourth volume of the *Manga*.

"This gathering together of the fruit of his labor has resulted in the present volume."

There were landscapes and figures, animals and utensils, and views of temples and pagodas.

One picture showed a shrine spread out over a hilly landscape dotted with dark pines. In the foreground was an enclosure surrounded by a wall, and on two distant hills the tiered roofs of two pagodas pointed toward the sky.

New volumes of the *Manga* appeared each year, but Hokusai never bothered to open the packets of money sent him by the publisher. When bill collectors called he handed out one of the packets lying on his table. If a tradesman found he was overpaid, he bowed and scraped and hastily left the room, but if he received too little he would return the next day for more.

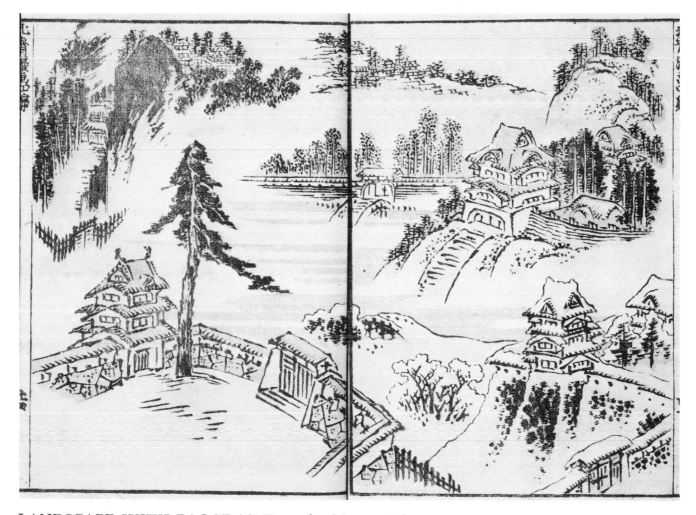

LANDSCAPE WITH PAGODAS. From the *Manga*, Volume 4

1816

The Metropolitan Museum of Art, New York

Gift of Howard Mansfield, 1936

"There can be no teacher in painting," Hokusai told the artists who asked him to teach them painting.

"All you need to do is copy reality," he remarked. But when artists begged the master to show them how to draw, he agreed to make more sketches.

Hokusai's thin people made the readers of the *Manga* laugh, for these poor undernourished men and women did not look unhappy. A blind man sat beside three women, one of whom was working on some kind of sewing. A cadaverous knight, or "samurai," holding a fan, sat beside his sword, and below two human skeletons played Japanese chess, while their skinny companion watched intently.

Many Japanese artists criticized the *Manga*, because it pictured vulgar subjects; but the people of Edo, who loved these lively sketches of themselves, continued to beg for more.

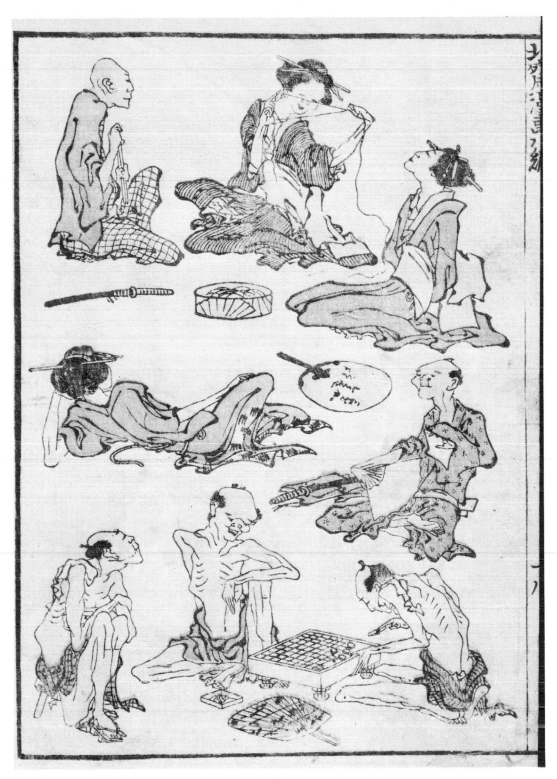

THIN PEOPLE. From the *Manga*, Volume 7

1817

The Metropolitan Museum of Art, New York

Gift of Howard Mansfield, 1936

The Japanese were ardent sportsmen. They admired their wrestlers, whose rugged training had made them fat and strong, and their acrobats who, after years of practice, could perform amazing tricks. Hokusai often watched these acrobats practicing contortions on the street. One page of the *Manga* showed an acrobat using his foot to place a basket on his head, another twisted one leg around his neck, and a third was practicing somersaults.

In the same book were sketches of wrestlers, jugglers, buildings, and detailed drawings of machines. This was the eighth volume of the *Manga* to be published in three years, and each was as popular as the one before. Hokusai's public waited impatiently for volume nine.

ACROBATS. From the *Manga*, Volume 8

1817

The Metropolitan Museum of Art, New York

Gift of Howard Mansfield, 1936

Volume nine offered new surprises.

"This time," wrote the author of the preface, "the artist has attempted to draw . . . the old battle scenes we hear of in tales . . . Opening the volume we are truly . . . in that actual world of old!"

One picture, stretching across two pages, showed an army winding its way through a mountainous, snowy landscape. In the right-hand corner of the drawing Hokusai had written a description of the scene. This was the army of a well-known Chinese Emperor which, after a long campaign, was marching home, "following the lead of an old horse." Hokusai had used a winter landscape as a setting for a human story. This picture of an army struggling through snow-covered mountains, told an awesome tale of nature dominating man.

LANDSCAPE OF ARMY IN SNOW. From the *Manga*, Volume 9

1817

The Metropolitan Museum of Art, New York

Gift of Howard Mansfield, 1936

Some pages of volume nine were alive with different kinds of people. Readers chuckled over one which showed only fat men: Two were busy doing laundry, while another took a bath. A wrestler, sitting cross-legged, held a fan on which was written "Victory." Below three genial pot-bellied men filled their buckets with water from a rain barrel.

FAT MEN. From the *Manga*, Volume 9
1817
The Metropolitan Museum of Art, New York
Gift of Howard Mansfield, 1936

The tenth volume of the *Manga* illustrated familiar tales. Some were events in history, some ghost stories and others tales of fantasy. One two-page spread illustrated a popular story about mice. Unlike the mice which scuttled about Hokusai's studio, these moved and dressed like men.

Hokusai's picture showed them working in the hideaway where they stored their money. Three were pulling in a sack of coins, three were weighing money, and three more kept the books. On the left the treasurer, sitting on a pile of bales, was busily adding on an abacus.

Hokusai's public had to wait fifteen years for another volume of the *Manga*. During these years, the master was busy turning out colored wood-block prints which were as popular as his drawings.

When Hokusai was seventy-four the eleventh volume of the *Manga* appeared in the Edo bookshops.

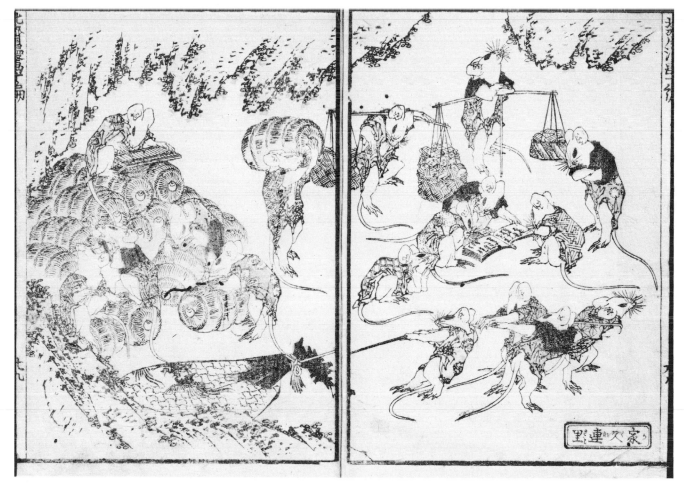

MICE. From the *Manga,* Volume 10

1819

The Metropolitan Museum of Art, New York

Gift of Howard Mansfield, 1936

"The master . . . again poises his brush," wrote the author of the preface to volume eleven, "and fills in the scenes he has neglected hitherto." These were drawings of great Japanese artists and of famous calligraphers noted for their skill in writing with a brush. On one page, Hokusai, a master of the brush, honored six brilliant craftsmen. One artist drew a horse which looked so alive that it ran away. A second, noted for his lettering, painted a big sign. A third wrote a poem on a tree trunk. A fourth observed a frog, and a fifth, named the "Five-Brush Monk," held brushes in his hands, feet, and mouth. At the foot of the page another famous monk drew with a broom held between his legs.

The last and fifteenth volume of the *Manga* was published many years after Hokusai had died.

"The master's remaining works are now completed," wrote the publisher. "My only wish now is that the world will take and love this book."

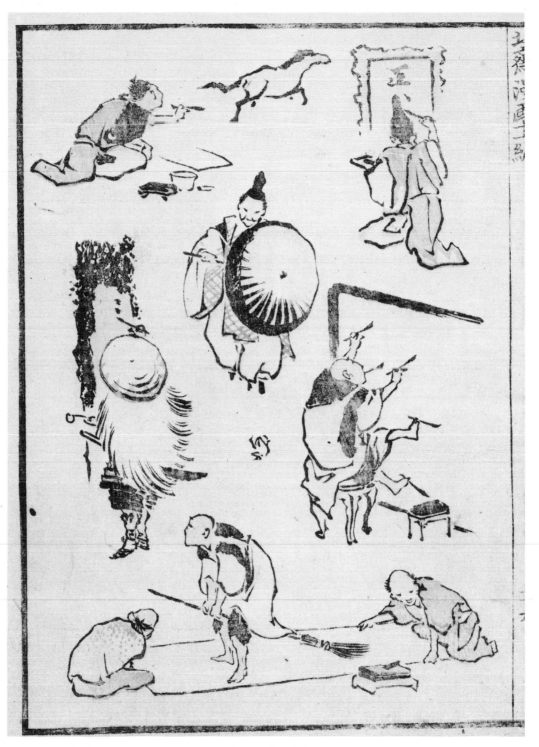

FAMOUS CALLIGRAPHERS. From the *Manga*, Volume 11

1834

The Metropolitan Museum of Art, New York

Gift of Howard Mansfield, 1936

Hokusai often used his drawings in the *Manga* as studies for his wood-block prints. Over and over he referred to his sketches when he designed a set of prints showing different views of Fuji. This cone-shaped, snow-capped mountain, climbed by pilgrims every year, was a sacred symbol of Japan, but Hokusai was the first artist to make it the subject of a picture. His *Thirty-six Views of Fuji* showed the mountain from many angles and in every kind of weather. Travelers, buffeted by a high wind, struggled along a road leading to the mountain. Men with knees bent clung to their bundles, while hats, papers, and leaves went sailing in the air. Two trees were bending under the fierce blast, while Fuji, silhouetted against the sky, appeared immovable and serene.

MOUNT FUJI SEEN FROM EJIRI. From *Thirty-six Views of Fuji*

1823–29. Wood-block Print. (9¾″ × 14½″)

Courtesy, Museum of Fine Arts, Boston

Some of Hokusai's views of Fuji showed the mountain seen from the Tokaido Road, some from a village, or over the roof-tops of a city. There were pictures of pilgrims climbing Fuji, and close-up views of the mountain's majestic summit. The red cone, sprinkled with white snow, rose above the clouds into a clear blue sky.

In many prints Fuji's snow-capped cone was barely showing above the horizon of the ocean. One view showed it framed in the curve of an enormous breaker which was about to crash on three fishing boats riding in the furrows. The fishermen crouched in terror, while Fuji in the distance appeared aloof and calm. Once again Hokusai pictured nature dominating man.

The *Thirty-six Views of Fuji* were as popular as the *Manga*, but Hokusai, now sixty-eight, was poor. Whenever he received money for his books or prints he cheerfully gave it to his worthless grandson, who was constantly in debt. He continued to move from house to house, and each was as shabby and dirty as the one before. He ate little and spent every daylight hour working in his studio.

One morning in 1828, Hokusai tried in vain to pull himself from the mat where he had been sleeping. Suddenly he realized that he was paralyzed. When his family urged him to call a doctor, he shook his head and announced that he would cure himself. He instructed his wife to prepare a drink according to an old Chinese recipe: Lemons were sliced a certain way, then boiled in an earthenware pot with a strong rice wine called "sake." In a few weeks Hokusai was cured and at work once more designing prints of well-known waterfalls.

THE GREAT WAVE. From *Thirty-six Views of Fuji*
1823–29. Wood-block Print. (10½″ × 15″)
Courtesy, Museum of Fine Arts, Boston

The Japanese loved their waterfalls which provided inspiration for poets and artists and picnic spots for travelers. Hokusai showed two picnickers sitting on a grassy ledge, beside a well-known waterfall. Nearby, their servant was preparing tea. Blue and white streaks of water fell from a hollow in the cliff above them.

This was the Amida waterfall, named for the Amida Buddha because, people thought, the shape of the hollow in the cliff resembled the head of a well-known Buddha statue.

It was not easy to give an effect of moving, translucent water in a wood-block print, for each subtle gradation of tone or color had to be printed from a separate block. Hokusai's waterfalls sometimes looked like solid white streaks flowing around rocks or cascading from great heights; but this set of prints was one of the most decorative he ever made.

AMIDA WATERFALL. From *Waterfall* Series

1827–30. Wood-block Print. (14¼″ × 10″)

Courtesy, Museum of Fine Arts, Boston

William S. and John T. Spaulding Collection

Hokusai's sketchbooks were filled with drawings of bridges, some curved like half-moons, some zigzagging across marshes, and others suspended across a gorge. He used these drawings when he designed a set of prints called *Famous Bridges*.

One print showed two porters with heavy loads picking their way across a primitive hanging footbridge. The trip was perilous, for the bridge, scarcely wider than a tightrope, gave under every step. Had one bearer lost his balance, both men would have plunged into the chasm far below.

Hokusai, who had often watched intrepid porters facing the perils of this bridge, wrote "Drawn from Nature" in the corner of the print. Once again he had pictured a contest between man and nature.

HANGING BRIDGE. From *Bridges* Series

1827–30. Wood-block Print. (9⅝″ × 14⅛″)

Courtesy, Museum of Fine Arts, Boston

Gift of William Sturgis Bigelow

Japanese houses were small and sparsely furnished. Instead of chairs people sat on cushions, and their beds were mats which were brought from the closet every night. The partitions were sliding paper screens and one side of the house opened on a garden. There was no wall space for pictures, but, built into every living room was a tiny alcove which contained one picture and a vase of flowers.

The Japanese women, trained in the art of arranging flowers, were able to make pleasing decorations with a few grasses or one spray of blossoms. Hokusai practiced the same economy when he designed a set of flower prints. Some showed a bird or butterfly hovering around a spray of blossoms, and others pictured only leaves and flowers.

One simple but striking composition showed two hanging clusters of blue wisteria against a rosy background. The tail of a gray bird in the lower right-hand corner, made a strong diagonal line across the page.

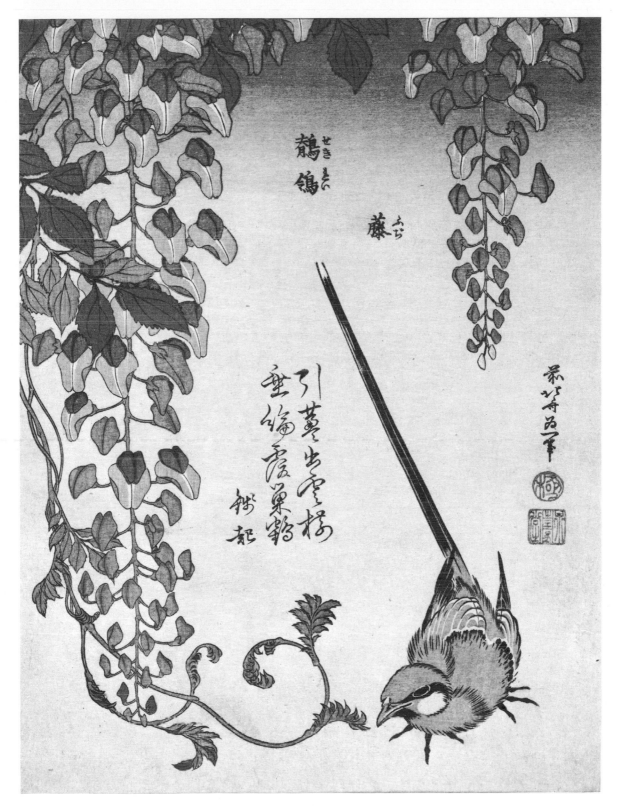

WISTERIA AND WAGTAIL. From *Small Flowers*

1830. Wood-block Print. (10⅛″ × 7½″)

Courtesy, Museum of Fine Arts, Boston

William S. and John T. Spaulding Collection

Ever since Hokusai was very young he had drawn different kinds of flowers. At seventy, he knew the formation of every leaf and blossom, but his flower prints never looked like stilted studies. His print of chrysanthemums, a favorite flower in Japan, was one of the handsomest in the "Large Flower" set. Although each leaf, stem, and blossom was precisely drawn, the different-size blossoms in shades of rose and orange made a bold pattern against a neutral background.

In one year Hokusai completed sixteen exquisite flower prints, but the harder he worked, the poorer he became. He continued to hand out money to his worthless grandson until, in 1834, Hokusai was bankrupt. When creditors threatened to arrest him, he changed his name, then went into hiding in Urawa.

CHRYSANTHEMUMS. From *Large Flowers*

1830. Wood-block Print. (10″ × 14⅝″)

Courtesy, Museum of Fine Arts, Boston

William S. and John T. Spaulding Collection

Hokusai nearly starved to death while he was in exile. What little money he earned was used to buy a fish shop for his grandson and to provide a wife to help him tend the store. He endured hunger and cold cheerfully, but he dreaded running out of paper, paints, and brushes. Sometimes, after dark, he would walk fifteen miles to Edo and return before daylight with a bundle of supplies.

"As to your 'old un,'" wrote seventy-four-year-old Hokusai to his publisher in Edo, "it is always the same, the power of the brush continues to grow." He advised the publisher about the printing of his *Book of Warriors*, giving minute instructions about how a wood block should be cut, and about the thickness and color of the ink.

"What I ask," wrote Hokusai, "is the sharpness of the engraver's execution, and this would be a satisfaction to a poor old man." On the same page he drew a picture of himself supported by two paint brushes instead of crutches.

Hokusai's *Book of Warriors* was published while he was in exile. In the preface he explained the purpose of the book.

"I find that in all Japanese and Chinese representations of war, force and movement are lacking. Regretting this defect, I am on fire to remedy it," wrote Hokusai.

The book was filled with pictures of fierce, angular warriors, some astride charging horses and others wielding mighty swords. Some were fighting demons and others evil beasts. One furious warrior, holding a long curved sword, was about to attack a great phantom bird which reared above him in the sky.

WARRIOR COMBATTING PHANTOM. From *Book of Warriors*

1836

Courtesy, Museum of Fine Arts, Boston

Hokusai was still in hiding when his book called *One Hundred Views of Fuji* appeared in the Edo bookshops. This picture book took the reader on a pilgrimage to Fuji. He saw the mountain through a summer shower, through a bamboo grove, and from an umbrella-maker's yard. Astronomers on a roof examined the mountain through a telescope; a poet, seeing Fuji from his window, threw up his arms in wonder; and a group of worshippers kneeling on the ground gazed adoringly at the calm massive cone above them.

"From the age of six I had a mania for drawing," Hokusai wrote in the preface to his book. "At seventy-three I had learned a little . . . in consequence when I am eighty I shall have made still more progress," he continued, "and when I am a hundred and ten, everything I do . . . will be alive." Hokusai, now seventy-five, signed the preface with his new name "Gwakio Rojin" or "Old Man Mad About Drawing."

"In this cruel season . . . there is nothing but hard times," Hokusai wrote his publisher, "but I am working furiously. My one aim is to become a great artist . . . As for my life it is no longer in the public eye and I cannot give you my address . . . I beg you to think of the sad condition in which I exist."

Hokusai had little to eat and only one thin kimono to keep him warm but when, after one year in hiding, he returned to Edo, he faced the same hardships he had endured in exile.

WORSHIPPERS AT THE FOOT OF FUJI. From *One Hundred Views of Fuji*

1834

Courtesy, New York Public Library

The crops failed in 1836, the year Hokusai returned to Edo. The starving Japanese had no money for prints and paintings, so Hokusai had to work day and night turning out cheap drawings which people could afford. For a few handfuls of rice he gave demonstrations of his skill. Sometimes he painted with a brush held in his mouth or between his toes, and sometimes, instead of a brush he used a bottle or an egg.

In spite of hardships, Hokusai remained cheerful; for, since the death of his second wife, his beloved youngest daughter, Oie, had come to keep him company. Because her little round pug face reminded him of a Pekinese dog, he nicknamed Oie, Chin-chin.

Chin-chin, a skilled artist herself, loved and understood her eccentric father. She never tried to clean his studio, and never allowed him to be interrupted in his work. She entertained his friends by telling fortunes while Hokusai continued drawing.

In 1837, Hokusai's house caught fire. Chin-chin and her father escaped with a few brushes, but all of Hokusai's drawings were destroyed. When friends sympathized with his loss, he shrugged his shoulders.

"I came into the world without much," he remarked, gazing at the pile of ashes which had been his home.

As soon as Hokusai had found another house he put to use the brushes he had saved. He drew a picture of himself at seventy-nine, old and bent, leaning on a cane. His neck was wrinkled, his jowls sagged, but his almond-shaped eyes gazed intently from under a furrowed brow.

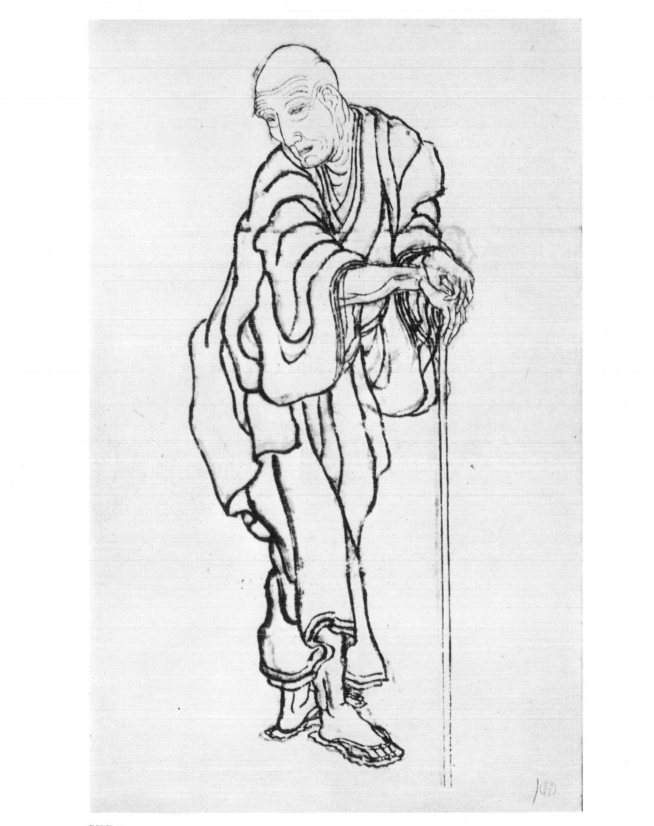

SELF-PORTRAIT. Drawing

1839

Musée Guimet, Paris

Photograph, Courtesy, New York Public Library

The older Hokusai grew, the harder he worked, hoping every day he would live long enough to perfect his drawing. He designed a picture book of famous heroes called *The Glories of China and Japan*, and at the same time he painted exquisite kakemonos, which were as sensitive and delicate as his illustrations were bold and strong. His compositions were simple and uncluttered. A willow branch, indicated by a few short brush strokes, and a flock of flying crows zigzagging downward, were all that Hokusai needed to make a pleasing picture.

In 1848, Hokusai moved again. In eighty-eight years he had lived in ninety different houses. His *Treatise on Color* was published that same year. It contained all that the artist had taught himself in eighty years. But in the preface Hokusai described the treatise as "only a cheap book for children."

WILLOW AND YOUNG CROWS

1842. Painting on Silk. (33⅜″ × 16¾″)

Courtesy, Museum of Fine Arts, Boston

"King Emma, The God of Hell . . . asks me to go and paint a kakemono for him," Hokusai wrote a friend in 1849. "I am thus obliged to leave, and when I leave, I shall carry my drawings with me. I am going to take a room at the corner of Hell Street and shall be happy to see you, whenever you pass that way." Hokusai, now eighty-nine, faced death as cheerfully as he had faced life's hardships.

Each day Chin-chin noticed that her father grew more feeble. She cooked him special dishes and saw that he kept his shoulders covered while he worked. All through the winter Hokusai sat huddled in his blanket painting kakemonos. One showed a bearded woodchopper leaning on his axe with bundles of faggots piled behind him.

When spring came Hokusai knew that he was dying. Lying on his mat, he called to Chin-chin to write down the verse he had composed, which, according to Japanese custom, would be inscribed upon his tombstone. Chin-chin dipped her brush in ink and wrote:

"My soul turned will-o'-the-wisp can come and go at ease over the summer fields." Hokusai smiled as he watched his daughter writing, then suddenly he realized that he would never hold a brush again. Reaching out his hand to Chin-chin he cried in anguish:

"If Heaven would grant me ten more years!" Then, gasping for breath he cried again:

"If Heaven would grant me *five* more years, I would become a real painter!" A few hours later Hokusai was dead. In eighty-nine years he had lived in ninety different houses and changed his name fifty times.

His ashes were buried in the graveyard of a monastery near his home. Friends placed flowers and incense in front of the tall narrow stone which marked his grave. Inscribed on one end was the poem he had written just before he died; on the other was a long list of family names. The only inscription on the face of the simple slab was the last of the fifty names chosen by Hokusai, it was:

"OLD MAN MAD ABOUT DRAWING."

A FAGGOT GATHERER

1849. Painting on Silk. (44⅞″ × 15⅞″)

Courtesy of the Smithsonian Institution, Freer Gallery of Art, Washington, D.C.

BIBLIOGRAPHY

Bowie, Theodore. *The Drawings of Hokusai*. Indiana University Press, Bloomington, Indiana: 1964.

Calkins, William Frederick. *Hokusai*. A Fable in Fact. Printed by B. Kennedy at the Gillick Press, Berkeley, California: [c. 1940].

Eckstein, Gustav. *Hokusai*. Play in fourteen scenes. Harper and Brothers, London and New York: 1935.

Focillon, Henri. *Hokusai*. Librairie Felix Alcon, Paris: 1925.

Hillier, Jack Ronald. *Hokusai*. Paintings, drawings, and woodcuts. Phaidon Press, London: 1955.

Hokusai. *The Thirty-six Views of Mount Fuji*. Heibonsha Ltd., Publishers, Tokyo. Distributed outside Japan by East-West Center Press, Honolulu.

Hokusai, The Man Mad on Drawing. With introduction by Joe Hloucha. Spring-Books, London: [c. 1960].

The Hokusai Sketchbooks, Selections from the *Manga* by James A. Michener. Charles E. Tuttle, Rutland, Vermont: 1958.

Holmes, C. J. *Hokusai*. Sign of the Unicorn, London: 1899.

Imman, Arthur Crew. *Three Moods: This I Know, Hokusai Saw, The Maples Are Red*. E. P. Dutton, New York: 1941.

Kondo, Ichitaro. *Katsushika Hokusai*. English text by Elise Grilli, based upon the Japanese text of Ichitaro Kondo. Charles E. Tuttle Co., Rutland, Vermont: 1956.

La Farge, John. *Great Masters*. McClure, Phillips and Company, New York: 1903.

Noguchi, Yoné. *Hokusai*. E. Mathews, London: 1925.

Strange, Edward F. *Hokusai, the Old Man with Painting*. Charles Scribner's Sons, New York: 1906.

INDEX

Amida Buddha, 52
Amida waterfall, 52
Amusements of the Eastern Capital, 20

Bakin, 22, 26
Book of Warriors, 60
Both Banks of the Sumida River at a Glance, 24
Buddha, 22, 30

Chin-chin, *see* Oie

Eastern Capital, 24
Edo, 6, 8, 10, 12, 16, 18, 20, 24, 30, 32, 36, 44, 60, 62, 64
Emperor of Japan, 18

Famous Bridges, 54
Fifty-three Stations of the Tokaido Road, 24
Fuji, 48, 50, 62

Glories of China and Japan, The, 66
Gwakio Rojin, *see* "Old Man Mad about Drawing"

Hell Street, 68
Hokusai, 16–40, 44–68
Holland, 14

Japan, 6, 14, 18, 22, 26, 30, 48

Kakemono, 16, 66, 68

Kano, 10
King Emma, God of Hell, 68
Kikujuro, 10
Kyoto, 18, 24

Large Flowers, 58

Manga, 30, 32, 34, 36, 38, 44, 46, 48, 50

Nagoya, 30
Nikko, 12

Oie (Chin-chin), daughter of Hokusai, 64, 68
"Old Man Mad About Drawing," 62, 68

Ronin, the forty-seven, 18

Samurai, 36
Shogun, 6, 14, 18, 32
Shunrō, 6, 8, 10, 12, 14, 24
Shunshō, 6, 8, 10, 12
Sōri, 14
Sumida River, 24
Surinomo, 14

Tactics of General Oven, The, 22
Thirty-six Views of Fiji, 48, 50
Tokaido Road, 24, 30, 50
Tokitara, 6
Treatise on Color, 66

Urawa, 58

921
HOKUSAI   21009

Ripley, Elizabeth

Hokusai; a biography